Julie Krone

THE ACHIEVERS

Julie Krone

Unstoppable Jockey

Jeff Savage

Lerner Publications Company • Minneapolis

To Nancy C. Savage and Nancy J. Savage for
their supreme love of animals

Information for this book was obtained from the following sources:
Ms., *New York Magazine, New York Times, Newsweek, People, Riding for my*
Life by Julie Krone with Nancy Ann Richardson, *Sports Illustrated, The New*
Yorker, The Sporting News, and *Women's Sports & Fitness.*

This book is available in two editions:
Library binding by Lerner Publications Company
Soft cover by First Avenue Editions
241 First Avenue North, Minneapolis, Minnesota 55401

International Standard Book Number: 0-8225-2888-6 (lib. bdg.)
International Standard Book Number: 0-8225-9728-4 (pbk.)

LIBRARY OF CONGRESS CATALOGING-IN-PUBLICATION DATA

Savage, Jeff, 1961–
    Julie Krone, unstoppable jockey / Jeff Savage.
        p.   cm. — (The achievers)
    Summary: Discusses the childhood, education, riding career, and
personal life of the first woman jockey to win a Triple Crown race.
    ISBN 0-8225-2888-6 (alk. paper)
    1. Krone, Julie. 2. Jockeys — United States — Biography — Juvenile
literature. 3. Women jockeys — United States — Biography — Juvenile
literature. [1. Krone, Julie. 2. Jockeys. 3. Women — Biography.]
I. Title II. Series
SF336.K76S28 1996
798.4'0092 — dc20
[B]   95-20676

Manufactured in the United States of America
1 2 3 4 5 6 – JR – 01 00 99 98 97 96

Contents

Julie Krone urges on Colonial Affair, at right, as they blast out of the starting gate at the 1993 Belmont Stakes.

1

Out in Front

Julie Krone stepped out of the stable into the chilly drizzle and announced that she was ready. Scotty Schulhofer smiled down at her. The trainer hoisted Julie onto the back of a king-size brown colt named Colonial Affair. Then Scotty playfully slapped the horse on his side. "You can do it!" he shouted to Julie as the huge horse trotted off.

Nearly 50,000 people had gathered in the rain at Belmont Park to witness the most important horse race in New York—the Belmont Stakes. Millions more were watching on television to see who would win horse racing's prestigious final race of the 1993 Triple Crown. Each year, the fastest three-year-old horses compete in a series of three races, together called the Triple Crown. The Kentucky Derby and the Preakness Stakes are the first two races of the Triple Crown.

Julie remembered watching the Belmont Stakes on television as a young girl. She had dreamed of someday being at the race. Now here she was, not just attending the event, but competing in it.

The horses clopped past the grandstand to the starting gate. One by one, the 13 horses were led into their starting stalls. Colonial Affair was in Stall 4, between speedy Kissing Kris and powerful Prairie Bayou, winner of the Preakness Stakes three weeks earlier. Julie lightly rubbed Colonial Affair's neck to relax him. Then she crouched into her riding position. At once, the bells clanged, the gates swung open, and the horses bolted off.

Mud spattered everywhere as the horses sped down the backstretch. Julie kept Colonial Affair to the back of the pack, hoping to save his energy for later. Suddenly, on the left, Prairie Bayou's knees buckled. Jockey Mike Smith bailed out over the horse's right side and fell to the track. Prairie Bayou trotted along a few steps more and then stopped. Something was wrong. Julie saw this, but she didn't know what had happened.

Julie kept Colonial Affair wide to stay clear of the mudslinging leaders. She knew that a horse gets discouraged if too much mud flies in its face. She yearned to pass the leaders but knew it would be a mistake to go all out too soon. Colonial Affair might run out of energy before the finish line.

Julie made sure Colonial Affair had enough energy to finish
the one and a half mile race with a burst of speed.

She chanted to herself over and over, "I have a ton of horse. I have a ton of horse."

Into the far turn, with half a mile to go, Julie could feel Colonial Affair wanting to go faster. "Now he's ready," Julie thought. Then she saw Sea Hero, another fast horse, make his move. If it's time for him, it's time for us, she thought.

Colonial Affair passed the other horses in the homestretch.

Around the far turn, she went wide. She urged her horse on, and he responded. Colonial Affair thundered down the track, surging past Wild Gate, past Sliver of Silver, past Cherokee Run, past the whole field at 40 miles an hour.

Down the homestretch, with Colonial Affair out in front, Julie looked back at the horses chasing her. "I am going to win the race I watched on TV when I was a kid!" she thought. "It's like a dream come true!"

Colonial Affair flew across the finish line first. Julie had done it!

An outrider pulled alongside her to lead her to the winner's circle. Tears rolled down Julie's mud-caked face. "How do you stop cryin'?" she asked.

Then Julie saw Bobby Duncan, leader of the starting-gate crew. "I won the Belmont, Bobby!" she said over and over. "I won the *Belmont!*" She sat aboard Colonial Affair as thousands of people shouted her name from the stands. "Julie! Julie! Way to go, Julie!"

Afterward, Julie called her mother, who had watched the race on television from Florida. "I'm on the ceiling," her mother told her. "Come scrape me off."

Julie's high spirits fell when she learned that Prairie Bayou, the horse that had stopped running, had suffered terrible damage to his left front leg.

Thirty minutes after the race, the racetrack veterinarian killed him as humanely as he could. "Destroying" a horse, as it is called, is common practice at racetracks when a horse breaks a leg. Racehorses' legs don't heal well or quickly. The horses are high-strung and hurt themselves even more trying to brush off a cast or other bandage. Julie was very sad when she learned of Prairie Bayou's death. "It's a heartbreaking thing," she said. "It's like losing a member of your family."

Prairie Bayou's accident was a sad ending to a triumphant day—the greatest day of Julie's life. She had already won more races than any female jockey in history. Now, aboard Colonial Affair, she had become the first woman to win a Triple Crown race.

Nearly everyone involved in horse racing is male. The horse's owner, the trainer who tends to the horse, the stablehands who help the trainer, and the jockey who rides the horse are almost always men or boys. Some people don't think women are strong enough to be jockeys. A jockey has to control a high-spirited horse that weighs more than 1,000 pounds. The jockey must be able to use his or her arms, hands, and legs to communicate with the horse and make it do what is needed. The jockey must also have quick reactions to guide a horse in a crowded race while the animals are running at about 40 miles an hour.

Trainer Scotty Schulhofer, left, didn't think women could be good jockeys until Julie Krone convinced him.

Scotty Schulhofer, Colonial Affair's trainer, was interviewed by reporters after the race. He admitted that for years he had been uncomfortable with women participating in horse racing. "When I learned that women wanted to ride, I was a little negative about it for some time," said the trainer. "It's just the idea of women competing against men."

And what, reporters asked Schulhofer, made him change his mind?

"Julie Krone," he said.

Horses have been special to Julie since she was a little girl.

2

Riding over the Rough Spots

Julie learned to ride on the back of her dog Twiggy before she could even walk. She was two years old when she rode a horse for the first time. It happened by accident. Julie's mother, Judi, raised horses and taught riding. Julie was sitting nearby as her mother tried to persuade a woman to buy one of the family's horses. "Look how sweet this horse is," Julie's mother said to the woman. "Look how gentle, how perfect for teaching your kids to ride." Without thinking, Judi lifted Julie and placed her on the horse's back. The horse trotted off. He arrived at the far wall of the indoor riding ring and stopped. Julie reached down, grabbed the reins, and tugged to one side. The horse turned around and trotted back to Julie's mother. Julie already seemed to have a special connection with horses.

By the age of four, Julie was riding ponies and horses almost every day, discovering their moods and ways. She learned plenty of rough lessons over the years. "I got bit, I got stepped on, I got kicked in the head," Julie remembers. "I got dumped five miles from home. The pony ran back and I had to walk."

Julie was born on July 24, 1963. She grew up in Eau Claire, Michigan, on a 10-acre farm overrun with chickens, goats, rabbits, turtles, and, of course, horses. Some neighbors complained that Julie ran wild. Really, she was just doing things that boys often did. One day Julie's father, Don, spotted her high up in a tree. He warned, "Better look out. You'll fall!" Julie replied, "I already did. Watch me climb."

Julie's fearless nature and love of horses came mostly from her mother. As a little girl, Judi tucked books about horses inside her schoolbooks so her parents and teachers wouldn't know what she was reading. But Judi grew up in an apartment in Chicago. There was no chance for her to actually ride a horse. Judi made sure her daughter would have an opportunity.

"Tuck your elbows in. Squeeze your knees tight. Keep your chin up." Julie's mother coached her on the fundamentals of riding. Julie won her first blue ribbon at the Berrien County Fair youth horse show, competing against teenagers in the 21-and-under division. Julie was five.

Julie took home a blue ribbon from the county horse show when she was five.

Her love of horses was limitless. She rode in the pasture each morning while waiting for the school bus. She went trick-or-treating on horseback. She learned to do tricks aboard horses that sent her father running for his camera. She even brought a horse into the house one time so that her mother could help her saddle it.

Julie became adept at dressage (dress SAUSH)—a slow, precise form of competitive riding. As a teen, she began competing in races and dressage events at fairs. She enjoyed show riding, but she loved the speed of racing more. When she was 14, she watched on television as a young jockey named Steve Cauthen won the Belmont Stakes aboard the horse Affirmed. "Mom," she declared, "I'm going to be a jockey!"

A year later, Julie's life took a painful turn. Her parents divorced. Julie's father and her older brother, Donnie, moved out of the house. She kept in touch with them, but her life wasn't the same. School became difficult as well. Classmates teased Julie for being small because she was just 4 feet 8 inches tall and weighed 90 pounds. She tried to appear older by wearing makeup, but the teasing just got worse. Her grades suffered.

Julie's passion for horses grew, however. She got up at six o'clock every morning to race her dark gray pony, Filly, through the snow alongside the road.

On her family's Michigan farm, Julie loved to do tricks with her ponies.

Steve Cauthen, just 18 years old, rode Affirmed, right, to victory in the 1978 Kentucky Derby. Cauthen and Affirmed also won the Belmont and the Preakness that year, earning horse racing's Triple Crown.

At night, she tied reins to her bed and pretended she was winning the Kentucky Derby.

In the spring of 1979, during a school vacation, Julie talked her mother into driving her to Louisville, Kentucky. Julie and her mother worked for a week as hotwalkers at Churchill Downs, the racetrack where the Kentucky Derby is held. Hotwalkers walk horses after they have run to cool them down. On the day before she returned home, Julie convinced a trainer named Clarence Picou to hire her as a groom and exercise rider for the summer.

Julie's summer was exciting but lonely. She lived with Clarence and his wife, Donna, in their home. When her workday was done, she often sat in a graveyard, hunched up against crooked tombstones, writing letters to her mother back in Michigan.

She kept busy at the track, though. There was something magical about being around racehorses. After they raced, Julie walked them alongside the track until their heart rates and temperatures returned to normal. She was convinced now that she wanted to be a jockey.

"I remember one day I worked a horse and came around the turn by the grandstand, riding him like he was Affirmed. In my mind I was winning the Kentucky Derby," Julie said. "Mr. Picou saw me and said, 'Hey, slow down. What do you think you're doing?' It was just an incredible feeling."

Churchill Downs, known for its twin spires, is one of the most famous tracks in horse racing.

Julie returned to Michigan for her junior year of high school, but she was frustrated. The other girls seemed to be interested only in clothes and boys. Julie had trouble concentrating on her schoolwork. She was obsessed with becoming a jockey.

Finally, the following summer, Julie got her chance. Her mother sent her 50 miles away to live with a family friend who owned and raced horses. He let Julie race some of his horses on the Michigan fair circuit. At fair circuits, unlike Churchill Downs and other big tracks, there is no betting on horses. Riders race for much smaller purses, or prize money, and the competition is easier. Julie finished second by the length of a horse's head in her first race. She quickly developed her racing skills. She rode in about 60 races. As she rode, she learned to break from the starting gate, ride in traffic, maneuver around turns, switch the whip from one hand to the other, and win.

School started again in the fall. For Julie, her senior year was no better than any other year. Her schoolmates still teased her. She decided she couldn't stand another year of it. She had to seek her true happiness. She had to be a jockey.

Julie and Filly won ribbons at the county fair.

3

Learning the Ropes

Julie dropped out of school three months into her senior year. Many jockeys had already been riding for a year by the time they were 17. Julie wanted to try professional racing. Although her father tried to persuade her to stay in school, Julie's mother agreed to let her quit. Julie hugged her mother good-bye and left for Florida to live with her grandparents, Carl and Marguerite Weber. The Tampa Bay Downs racetrack was near their home. Julie would pursue her dream of becoming a jockey there.

The guard at the gate, however, wouldn't let her enter. Julie had a folder full of photos her dad had taken of her racing horses in Michigan. The guard wasn't impressed. He told her the track was no place for a little girl. So Julie walked around the corner and hopped over the fence.

She was picked up by a woman in a car who thought Julie was lost. The woman took her to see her friend, a trainer named Jerry Pace. "So," the trainer said, "I'm told you want to be a jockey."

"No," Julie said. "I'm *going* to be a jockey."

Jerry was amused and curious. He put Julie on a horse and watched her ride. He was impressed. "I'm going to put you on your first winner," he announced.

Racehorses are expensive animals to buy and to maintain. The owner of a racehorse hires a trainer to take care of it. The trainer hires a jockey to ride the horse in a race. A jockey hires an agent to find rides and negotiate the jockey's pay.

The owner pays a fee to enter a horse in a race. The money from all the owners with horses in the race, plus some money from the track, is called the purse. The purse is divided among the first three horses in a race, with the winning horse's owner earning the most. A jockey earns about 10 percent of the purse awarded to the horse's owner. The jockey pays the agent about 10 percent of the jockey's earnings.

A trainer also earns a percentage of the purse. A trainer usually has horses from several owners in his or her stable. When a horse wins, the owners are happy and more owners want to hire that trainer.

Julie arrived at the racetrack each morning at dawn. She fed Jerry's horses and waited for the opportunity to race. She rode the horses in their workouts. She earned her jockey's license by showing the track stewards that she could control a horse.

On January 30, 1981, she got her first chance to race. She trotted onto the track aboard a horse named Tiny Star. Julie wore her racing silks—white pants with her name sewn in the back, and a blouse and peaked cap in the colors of the horse's owner— for the first time.

Julie guided Tiny Star to a second-place finish. Julie might have won aboard Tiny Star had she been permitted to use a crop, or short whip. As a beginning jockey, Julie could not use a crop in her first three races.

Beginning jockeys do have one advantage over more experienced jockeys, however. One year after a jockey wins his or her fifth race, the jockey becomes an apprentice jockey. The jockey is an apprentice jockey for one year. All horses in a race are required to carry a certain amount of weight, including the jockey and saddle. The track officials decide how much weight each horse should carry so that the race is fair and competitive. Beginning and apprentice jockeys get a weight allowance, which means that the horses they ride carry less weight than the other horses in the race. After a jockey wins a certain number of races within a certain period of time, usually a year, he or she is no longer an apprentice jockey.

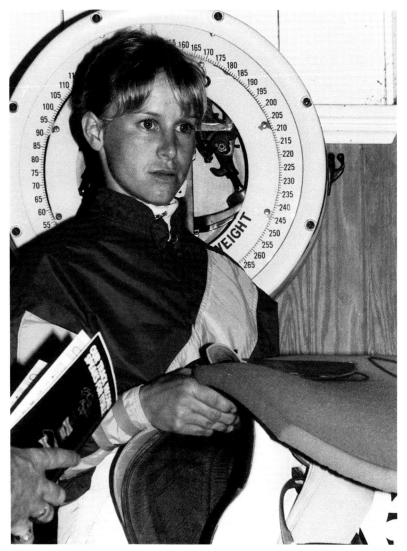

Julie weighs in before a race. A jockey and his or her equipment is weighed before each race to make sure the horse will be carrying the correct amount of weight.

Two weeks after her first race, Julie won for the first time. Riding an older horse named Lord Farkle, she took the lead around the final turn and held it. "I kept waiting for somebody to pass me," she said. No one did.

Julie won three of her next six races, then won aboard Lord Farkle again. She was on her way now. She had a good riding style and was good with horses. Some of the other owners began letting her ride their horses.

Julie had heard other jockeys talk about a former jockey named Julie Snellings, who worked in the racing secretary's office. Julie Snellings's office was downstairs, below the jockeys' locker room where Julie had a private room in which to change clothes. Other jockeys began to pass along suggestions from Julie Snellings. They told Julie when Julie Snellings said she should ride differently or change her style. Once Julie started winning, she developed plenty of confidence—maybe too much. After a while, Julie decided Julie Snellings was giving her too much advice. She burst into Julie Snellings's office. "If you know so much, why don't you ride?" Julie snapped.

Julie Snellings rolled out from behind her desk in a wheelchair. Julie was stunned. She didn't know what to say. She learned then that Julie Snellings's legs had been paralyzed in 1977, her only year of racing, when a horse had fallen on her.

Lord Farkle was Julie's first winning mount.

One day, Julie showed up at the track wearing Julie Snellings's old racing outfit. It was four years to the day after the accident that had left Snellings paralyzed. Snellings was surprised and touched that her friend would honor her, but she was also terrified that something might happen to Julie. Something did happen. Julie won three races in one day for the first time in her life. "She was so tough," Julie Snellings said, "so determined not to let anything in the world get in her way."

Several races are held each day over several weeks in what is known as a racing meet. When the racing meet at Tampa Bay Downs ended, Julie needed a new place to ride. Other meets around the country were about to begin, including the meet at Pimlico Racetrack in Baltimore, Maryland. Julie Snellings convinced her former agent, Chick Lang, to help the 17-year-old apprentice rider at Pimlico.

Chick did his best to get Julie work, but most trainers didn't want a woman to ride their horses. "Nobody took girl riders seriously—they were a joke," one trainer said. "Nobody thought a girl was strong enough. It ate Julie up to be considered a girl jockey."

Back in 1969, Diane Crump and Patricia Barton had become the first women to compete as full-time jockeys. Not everyone appreciated their achievement. Some horse racing experts had scoffed.

Diane Crump, right, was the first American woman to ride at a track where betting was allowed.

Nick Jemas, head of the Jockeys' Guild, had said women were bad for the sport. "They won't last," he said. "They're not strong enough to become good race riders. They'll freeze. They'll panic. This is no game for girls."

Other women had competed as jockeys from time to time. They had endured insults from other jockeys and some fans. Patricia Barton had ridden hundreds of winners during a 15-year career that was plagued by harassment from male opponents.

Julie did her best to fit in with the men at the track. She didn't wear makeup. She didn't comb her hair or wear it in a ponytail. She didn't smile, even when she was in the winner's circle. She walked and talked like a boy. She even spat like one.

She pleaded with owners and trainers to let her ride. She brought doughnuts for them and carrots for their horses. She shook hands with a firm grip to show how strong she was. She compared herself to legendary jockey Willie Shoemaker. Trainers would ask how big she was. "Four-foot-ten-and-a-half, 102 pounds," she would say, standing on her toes, "same as Shoemaker."

Mounts still were hard to find. So she rode mostly "long shots"—horses that weren't likely to win. After two months at Pimlico, she had won just five times. She was ready to go back to her mother in Michigan. Then she met Bud Delp, a big-time trainer.

4

Breaking into the Big Time

Bud Delp was an expert trainer with a stableful of fast horses. He knew a good jockey when he saw one. Too young? Too small? A girl? It didn't matter to Bud. He hired Julie to ride his horses. But there was a catch. Julie had to sign up with a new agent—Bud's son, Gerald Delp. Accepting a new agent meant Julie had to drop Chick Lang. Julie struggled with the idea until Chick insisted that she sign with the Delps.

Julie performed as Bud knew she would. She rode winner after winner at Pimlico, then went with Bud to Delaware Park and kept on winning. In one four-month stretch, she brought in more than 100 winners.

On February 26, 1982, Julie broke a Maryland record by becoming the first female jockey in the state to win four races in one day. But Julie didn't want just the "female" records, she wanted to break all the records.

Riding was still a lonely business for Julie. Many of the male jockeys resented her. She seldom got a chance to see her mother or father. She spent nearly every waking hour with horses. The loneliness seemed worth it to Julie, though. Her dreams were coming true. She lived in a nice apartment in Baltimore and was earning good money.

Then she nearly threw it all away. Pimlico track officials suspected Julie was getting into trouble. They searched her car one day and found a marijuana joint in her ashtray. She was not arrested, but she was suspended from racing for 60 days. Julie also had to go through a drug-treatment program. She struggled to overcome her addiction to marijuana, which had started when she was growing up in Michigan.

For the first time that Julie could remember, she wasn't allowed to ride a horse. She peered through the fence at Pimlico every day, thinking about her mistake, yearning to ride again. "I was very depressed," she said. "It was pure torture. I was young, but that was no excuse for being stupid."

Julie decided she could give up drugs but she couldn't stop riding. Chick Lang agreed to be her agent again. When her suspension ended, several trainers gave her a second chance by letting her ride their horses. On her first day back, she had two races. She won both.

One of the trainers who gave her another chance was Steve Brown. Later, Julie and Steve began to date. Sometimes they went to hockey games. Julie enjoyed having fun away from the racetrack. But trouble found her once again. Julie was exercising one of Steve's horses, a chestnut filly, at Laurel Racetrack when a support bandage on the horse's front leg unwound. The horse fell and Julie was tossed into the air. She landed on her back. "I was looking up at the sky and I couldn't move my legs," she said.

Julie was rushed by ambulance to the hospital. She had broken her back.

Doctors ordered Julie to stay off horses and rest for three months. Julie couldn't imagine such a thing. She broke down and cried in the emergency room. She spent painful days and nights flat on her back, fearing that her life as a jockey was over. But she was determined to ride again. She exercised daily, enduring the pain it took to regain her strength. She wore a back brace while out of bed. At last, after many weeks, doctors said she could return to the track.

She left Maryland and went to the Atlantic City Race Course in New Jersey. In her first race, she dropped her whip but still won by a head. The victories just kept coming. Julie went on to win the riding title. She rode more winners in the two-month meet than any male jockey at the track.

Julie couldn't get enough. Since the Atlantic City track operated at night, she raced during the day at nearby Monmouth Park. She woke up at dawn, galloped horses in the morning, raced at Monmouth in the afternoon, then rode at Atlantic City in the evening, and finally got to bed well after midnight. To save time, she would prepare for the next day by tucking her pant legs and some socks into her boots so she could hop out of bed straight into her clothes.

She won the racing title at Atlantic City again in 1983, but she lost her boyfriend. One day, Steve ended their relationship. Julie's first love came to a screeching halt. Not only was Julie's heart broken, suddenly she couldn't seem to win any more. She didn't win one of her next 80 races. She was so frustrated that in one race she screamed "I quit! I quit!" all the way down the backstretch.

But Julie did not quit. She tried harder than ever to pull out of her slump. Eventually her work began to pay off. She started winning again. She won at Monmouth. At Pimlico. At The Meadowlands in New Jersey. She packed her suitcase, her three teddy bears, and her cat, Skaggs, into her car and moved from track to track, wherever the horses were running. Nothing would stop her. Nothing.

For a while, Julie stopped winning but she didn't stop trying.

5

Back in the Saddle

The telephone rang one day in 1986. It was Julie's mother. A few years earlier, Judi Krone had moved to Florida and bought a satellite TV dish so she could watch Julie's races. But Judi wasn't calling to offer congratulations. Something was terribly wrong. Judi told her daughter that she had cancer in her abdomen. The doctors said she had only two years to live, even with surgery and radiation treatments. Julie couldn't believe it.

Julie helped her mother the only way she knew how. She won races. She climbed aboard horses, powered them down the track to the finish line, jumped off, and hollered to anyone nearby, "Call my mom and tell her I won!" She mailed videotapes of her winning races to her mother, who had moved into a lodge for cancer patients. Some days, Julie won three times. Some days, four. Some days, five.

In 1986, she won 199 times. In 1987, she won a record-breaking 324 times. She won six times in one day. At Monmouth, she won 50 races more than anyone else. In two years, Julie had earned more than $700,000.

Then one day, Julie heard news that topped all the victories and all the money: Judi's cancer had been successfully treated, the doctors said. Julie's mother was going to live.

By now, Julie was ranked as the sixth-best jockey in the entire country. Male jockeys who didn't like losing to a female were bitter about Julie's success. For every jockey like Chris Antley, a friend of Julie's, she had plenty of enemies. Yves Turcotte whipped Julie's horse across the head in a race at Pimlico. After the race, Julie shoved Yves off the weigh-in scale. Jake Nied challenged Julie to a fight in the jockeys' room after a race at Keystone. They grappled before other jockeys managed to separate them. After Julie breezed to a win by 10 lengths one day, Miguel Rujano rode up beside her and smacked her across the face with his whip. During the photo session afterward, Julie noticed her ear was bleeding. "Excuse me," she said politely. "I have to go hit somebody." She walked up to Miguel and punched him in the nose. He threw her into the pool. She clobbered him over the head with a lawn chair. Nobody intimidated Julie Krone.

Chris Antley and Julie became friends when they both raced in Atlantic City. They are still good friends despite racing against each other.

Angel Cordero, one of the greatest jockeys ever, remembered when Julie began showing up regularly in the jockeys' room. "There was a time when you'd hear whispering in the corner," said Angel, who never doubted Julie's ability. "The only way you stop the whispering is by winning. That's what Julie did."

Julie rode five winners in one day at Monmouth in 1988, but she had done even better the year before when she had a six-win day.

Even winning did not stop some jealous riders, however. Julie was driving toward her 1,200th career victory when the jockey she was about to pass down the stretch reached out and yanked her horse's reins. Her horse almost fell as Julie clung desperately to his neck. The jockey, Armando Marquez, claimed that his hand accidentally got tangled in Julie's reins. The stewards at Garden State Park awarded Julie the victory and suspended Armando for six months.

Larry Cooper, who had become Julie's agent in 1983 when she moved to New Jersey, saw Julie get bullied for many years. "I think it happens, maybe because she's a girl," Larry said. "Maybe some of the guys are frustrated and they take it out on her."

Not all jockeys dislike Julie. Some male jockeys admire her. "I don't look at her as a 'girl' rider," jockey Richard Migliore said. "She's a girl—that's obvious. But she's a good rider. And that's the highest compliment I can pay her, because up until now there really haven't been any girls I could say that about."

In November 1988, Julie became the first female jockey to compete in the Breeder's Cup—an afternoon of racing in which each event is worth more than $1 million. Although she finished fourth aboard Forty Niner in her only race of the day, she was happy just to compete with the world's best.

Julie was the leading rider with two weeks left in the 1990 Monmouth meet in New York when she suffered a bizarre injury. She was galloping a horse during an exercise ride when the horse bucked. Julie was thrown forward over the horse's head. She landed on her feet, still holding the reins. Snap! She heard it before she felt it. Then the pain surged through her leg and she fell to the ground. "Hey, I just broke my ankle!" she yelled to a trainer. Her agent, Larry Cooper, was at her side in an instant. He drove her to the hospital, where she was fitted with a cast.

Julie went to the beach at Nantucket to rest. Three days later, Larry called to tell her that another jockey needed just 10 victories to catch her in the Monmouth standings. Julie tore off her cast that day, had a doctor put on a smaller cast that would fit into her riding boot, and returned to Monmouth for the rest of the meet. She won the riding title despite a broken ankle.

By now, Julie was a fabulous success story. She appeared as a guest on television programs such as *Late Night with David Letterman* and *The Tonight Show*. She was even invited to the White House to meet President George Bush.

Being famous was exciting, but Julie still enjoyed riding above all. She won more titles in New Jersey and New York. At Belmont Park in 1992, she led all riders in the spring meeting with 73 victories. She earned $920,000 in two months of racing. She also rode in the Kentucky Derby.

Julie raced at Gulfstream Park in Florida in the spring of 1993, then returned to New York to compete in the Belmont Stakes on June 5. As she trotted from the stable toward the track aboard Colonial Affair, Julie leaned forward and whispered to the horse, "Let's go out and make some history." They did. By guiding the big bay colt first across the finish line, Julie became the first woman ever to win a Triple Crown race.

Julie moved to nearby Saratoga Race Course for the summer. There, she consistently won races against some of the best jockeys in the world. She set another milestone with her 2,500th career victory. Many racing fans and trainers considered Julie to be horse racing's hottest jockey. But on the final day of racing at Saratoga, disaster struck once again.

In 1993 Julie became one of three jockeys to win five races in one day at the Saratoga Race Course.

Julie's success and her outgoing personality make her a favorite with racing fans.

Coming around the final turn on top of the favorite, Seattle Way, Julie was about to make her move. Then, suddenly, another horse cut sharply to the right. "No! No!" Julie screamed as she stood. It was too late. Seattle Way crashed into the other horse. Julie was catapulted, head over heels, through the air. She landed hard on her ankle in the middle of the track. A kicking hoof slammed into Julie's chest and knocked her into a somersault.

"It hurt so bad, I felt like I was in outer space," Julie said. "I couldn't breathe. I kept thinking, 'Pass out. Please, pass out.' But I didn't."

Julie was rushed to Saratoga Hospital. Doctors cared for her while she screamed in pain for five hours. Her elbow socket was cracked and protruding from her skin. Her heart was bruised. Her two major leg bones, the tibia and fibula, were broken. Her ankle was shattered to bits. If she hadn't been wearing a protective jacket, which is similar to a bulletproof vest, doctors guessed that the blow to her chest would have killed her. As it was, her ankle was broken in more places than anyone could count. The next day, she was flown to another hospital where two metal plates and 14 screws were inserted into her ankle.

Such a terrible crash would end the career of many jockeys. Not Julie. Nothing stops her. Not operations or needles. Not casts or crutches. Not wheelchairs or pain. Julie fought through it all just so she could ride again. Her family and friends encouraged and comforted her while she was in the hospital for a month. Angel Cordero visited her often, as did other jockeys and trainers. She spent much of her time reading letters from fans. She received 80 pounds of mail in a month.

On May 25, 1994, after nine months of painful therapy, Julie Krone came back. She climbed aboard a dark brown horse named Baypark, broke slowly out of the gate, then charged hard down the stretch into third place amid the cheers of thousands of fans at Belmont Park. The next day, on top of a dark bay filly named Consider the Lily, Julie crossed the wire first. The fans erupted. "Way to go, Julie!" they screamed. "Julie, you're back!"

Julie's comeback at the track was stunning, but it was also slow. During the 1994 racing season, she didn't compete in as many races as she usually did. That November she had surgery to remove the plates and pins that had helped her ankle heal. But just two months later, while racing at a track in Florida, Julie fell again. This fall was not as harmful as the last one, however, and before long, Julie was riding again. She recovered so well that she was able to ride Suave Prospect in the 1995 Kentucky Derby. Although they finished 11th, Julie was glad to be back on the track.

Eight months after her horrible fall, Julie was back, exercising horses at Belmont Park. A month later, she won again.

Julie and Matt Muzikar were married in August of 1995.

As Julie continued her comeback, she was also busy planning her wedding to television sportscaster Matt Muzikar. Julie and Matt had met five years earlier when Matt was a security guard at Saratoga Race Course.

Although Julie's reputation as a winning jockey was well known, she didn't take any time off for her wedding. She rode in races the day of the ceremony and the day after it. "Whether you're a girl or a boy or a Martian," Julie says, "you still have to go out and prove yourself again every day."

Julie Krone always wanted to be a jockey. Not a "girl" jockey. Not a "female" jockey. Just a jockey.

She had no idea she would be breaking so many barriers along the way.

"Are you kidding me?" she says. "It never entered my mind. I was always going to be a jockey. And a great one, too."

Julie Krone's Career

Statistics

YEAR	STARTS	WINS (%)	SECONDS (%)	THIRDS (%)	HORSE'S EARNINGS
1981	747	124 (17)	106 (14)	120 (16)	$796,773
1982	1,049	155 (15)	150 (14)	146 (14)	$1,238,161
1983	1,024	151 (15)	140 (14)	138 (13)	$1,095,662
1984	801	108 (13)	95 (12)	121 (15)	$785,982
1985	1,041	106 (10)	140 (13)	119 (1)	$1,060,352
1986	1,442	198 (14)	209 (14)	182 (13)	$2,353,336
1987	1,698	324 (19)	270 (16)	247 (15)	$4,511,191
1988	1,958	363 (19)	321 (17)	273 (14)	$7,770,314
1989	1,673	368 (22)	287 (17)	235 (14)	$8,031,445
1990	634	142 (22)	120 (19)	81 (13)	$2,577,727
1991	1,414	230 (16)	229 (16)	188 (13)	$7,748,007
1992	1,445	278 (19)	243 (17)	190 (13)	$9,189,148
1993	1,012	212 (21)	171 (17)	136 (13)	$6,417,269
1994	570	101 (18)	85 (15)	79 (14)	$3,981,939
Totals	**16,710**	**2,902 (17)**	**2,613 (16)**	**2,282 (14)**	**$59,439,935**

Average performance for all jockeys: first-place finishes, 6 percent; second-place finishes, 7 percent; third-place finishes, 8 percent.

Julie gets about 10 percent of what the horse she rides in a race earns.

Highlights

- First woman to win a Triple Crown race, the 1993 Belmont Stakes
- First woman to win five races in one day at Saratoga Race Course
- First woman to compete in a Breeder's Cup race
- Leading jockey at The Meadowlands for four consecutive years (1987–1990)
- Won six races in one day at Monmouth Park and The Meadowlands
- Won five races in one day at Saratoga Race Course
- One of top 12 jockeys in earnings for four years
- Fourth woman to ride in the Kentucky Derby

Glossary

agent: A person who finds horses for a jockey to ride and negotiates the jockey's pay. An agent usually receives 10 percent of a jockey's earnings.

apprentice: A beginning jockey. When a jockey wins a certain number of races within a set period of time, he or she is no longer an apprentice jockey.

backstretch: The part of a race course opposite the finish line.

dressage: A competitive event in which a horse performs precise movements in response to subtle commands from its rider.

exercise rider: A person hired by a horse's trainer to gallop the horse each day on the racetrack and occasionally run it at close to top speed in a workout.

groom: A person hired by a trainer to feed and bathe horses and clean stalls.

hotwalker: A person hired by a trainer to walk alongside the horse after its workout until the horse's heart rate returns to normal.

mount: A horse ridden in a race. Also, the act of climbing on a horse.

outrider: A person riding a horse that is not in the race, who escorts the competing horses off the track after the race.

owner: A person who owns a horse, hires a trainer to care for it, and enters it in races.

purse: The amount of money available to be won in a race. The winner's purse often is about half the total purse.

racing meet: The season for races at a racetrack.

racing silks: The colored cap and jersey a jockey wears in a race. Each stable has a registered color, which the jockey wears when riding that stable's horses.

stewards: State officials who judge close races, decide when fouls have occurred, and discipline offenders.

trainer: A person who supervises the care and training of a horse or a stableful of horses. A trainer is hired by a horse's owner.

weight allowance: An advantage given to apprentice jockeys. The horses ridden by apprentice jockeys are allowed to carry less weight, usually a few pounds, than the horses they compete against.

workout: A training session in which a horse is run by the exercise rider on the racetrack at close to top speed. Workouts usually are held about every five days.

ACKNOWLEDGMENTS

Photographs are reproduced with the permission of: pp. 1, 13, 28, 34, 40, 52, 56, Bill Denver/Equi Photo; p. 2, Sportschrome/Ron Wyatt; pp. 6, 9, 10, 20, 32, 47, 51, AP/Wide World; pp. 14, 17, 19, 24, D. R. Krone; p. 22, Courtesy of Churchill Downs, Inc.; p. 30, Tom Cooley Photos; pp. 39, 43, 44, 48, Mark Wyville.

Front cover photograph by Mark Wyville. Back cover photograph by Bill Denver/ Equi Photo. Artwork by John Erste.